Laurence Dunn's

THAMES SHIPPING

Published by
Carmania Press
Unit 212, Station House, 49 Greenwich High Road, London SE10 8JL, Great Britain.

ISBN 0 9518656 1 7

British Library Cataloguing for Publication Data. A Catalogue Record for this book is available from the British Library.

Production by John Cocking and Roger Hardingham
Printed by The Amadeus Press, Cleckheaton,

First published November 1992
Second (revised) edition, April, 1994
Reprinted January, 1997
Reprinted January, 2001

Introduction

Much has been written about the beauties of the Upper Thames, but this book aims instead to show something of the life of the lower reaches and the pattern of shipping on this busy stretch of water, known to seafarers as London River. It has its own charms, but these are often in the eye of the beholder conditioned to see them.

The pictures which follow represent a personal collection and they bridge a period of some fifty years - from the days when London was the world's greatest port. They start at Hampton, 20 miles above London Bridge and where Thornycrofts - once world-famous - had one of their several shipyards. They continue down to London Bridge (the generally accepted measuring point), past the Upper Pool and then, via the various reaches and dock systems, to Gravesend - still regarded as the gateway to the port of London. They end in the estuary where, on Shivering Sands Fort, London's outermost Tidal Gauge is sited, this at a point 59 miles below London Bridge.

Inevitably over this span of time vast changes have taken place. Countless up-river wharves have ceased to exist, just a few being replaced by new ones designed to meet current needs. But always the trend has been to move further downstream, the traffic once handled by the various long-familiar dock systems now being mainly concentrated at Tilbury which, besides its important container and ro-ro traffic, handles grain, forest products and a range of other cargoes.

Traditional types of vessels, ranging from the once ubiquitous lighters and steam coasters to the conventional tramp, cargo liner or passenger ship have disappeared, some to reappear in much modified form as ro-ro, container or cruise ships, their numbers fewer but their size very much greater. The once numerous colliers have likewise shrunk in numbers but grown in individual capacity, while the size of tankers, after showing a dramatic increase, has since stabilised.

Each and every major port in Europe fights to maintain or improve its position, but the Thames and its trade have been plagued by adherence to restrictive practices, for instance the dockers' jobs for life concept - now fortunately no more - and the dangers which result from monopoly. London's decline from being the world's greatest port has been due to many causes, but much of it springs from the replacement of local competition by monopoly and the belief that charges can always be raised. The docker's bicycle has been replaced by the Mercedes while, to keep in step, the fare for the Tilbury-Gravesend ferry crossing has risen from a few pence to well over £1 each way.

All save a very few of the pictures were taken by myself, the others by my close friends Graeme Maclennan and the late Jeffery Curtis. To those who have scanned the text for possible errors or omissions I offer my most grateful thanks.

NOTE: The distances are quoted in land miles. The brackets after a ship's name contain first the date of her completion and then her tonnage. Gross tonnage is implied throughout unless otherwise stated. To further historical interest, the pictures - where possible - are dated, usually at the end of each caption.

At Wm Cory's barge repair works at Charlton.

The Upper Reaches

Hampton, Kingston, Richmond, Chiswick, Hammersmith Bridge, Putney, Chelsea, Little Venice, Westminster, Victoria Embankment, London Bridge, Upper Pool, Tower Bridge.

Thames Launches' cream hulled *Viscount* (1908/69) seen nearing Richmond after a 1960 trip from Westminster. Built by Salter Bros at Oxford, she was converted from steam to diesel in 1948. 106ft in length, she had an up-river passenger capacity of 395.

FROM RURAL TRANQUILITY
TO COMMERCIAL ACTIVITY

Above: This peaceful scene at Hurley typifies the serenity of the upper reaches of the Thames. However, for the first real links with vessels which belong to the busy lower reaches and the sea itself, one has to come some 39 miles downstream to Hampton.

Left: One of the more unusual vessels to be built by Thornycroft's Hampton yard was the 75 ft *John Ashley* which was launched in May 1958 for the Missions to Seamen. Her link with the London River was unique, since her role was to attend to the welfare and spiritual needs of seamen visitors to the port, her 'parish' extending to Gravesend and beyond - the area covered by this book.

About 45 miles separate the Hampton launch scene from these pictures taken from Tilbury Lock in 1982. In the upper view as one ship, the *City of London*, leaves so another is manoeuvred towards the lock entrance by the tugs *Sun Swale* (centre) and *Hibernia*. In the scene below a large container ship starts her voyage just as a Russian timber carrier nears her destination. The tall chimneys are those of the Blue Circle Northfleet cement works. The tug *Avenger* (1963/292) was subsequently sold to Canada.

DOWNSTREAM FROM KINGSTON

Above: The Royal Princess (1935/115) seen off Kingston in 1969 was the first of London's large upstream excursion boats to be diesel driven. She had a passenger capacity of 500 and was built at Rowhedge, Essex, for A Crouch & Co., London who later sold her to Thames Launches Ltd., of Teddington.

Left: Although the Thames is tidal as far as Teddington Lock there is a half-tide weir at Richmond. Raised two hours before high water to admit the top of the tide, it is lowered four hours later to retain the water at a convenient level. Immediately below the weir the rise and fall is considerable - up to 21.5 feet - and even this flat-bottomed barge was probably touching the river bed. However, at half-tide traffic begins to move again.

Top Right: Due to their seasonal employment most of the up-river vessels have had long lives. However, winter can bring its hazards and during the floods of March 1964 the 52-ton *Princess Beatrice* was one of three torn from their moorings at Eel Pie Island and smashed against Richmond Bridge. Then something of a veteran, she had been built at Hampton in 1896.

Centre Right: Funnel down! In the days of steam the tall funnel had to be lowered for each and every bridge. The *Abercorn* (1925/92) - later converted to diesel - was the second of three sisters built at Oxford. Designed to carry some 375 passengers apiece, their hulls, long and shallow, measured 115 ft overall x 16 ft 9 ins beam, but had a draught of only 3 ft (1947).

Below: The *Viscountess* (1926/83) seen off Syon in 1959 after she had been converted from steam to diesel. Built at Oxford, she and her sisters *Abercorn* and *Queen Elizabeth* were first owned by Mears' of Richmond and then by Thames Launches. For long the largest and finest in these fleets, they operated from Westminster to points up-river such as Kew, Richmond and Kingston

KEW TO HAMMERSMITH

Left: The British motor coaster *Edna B* (1938/242) nears Strand-on-the-Green (just below Kew Bridge) inward bound from Antwerp for Isleworth, the upper limit for such vessels. Dutch-built craft of this type were of shallow-draught and so could reach up-river wharves denied to older steam driven coasters. (1973).

Below: One of several training ships once moored up-river was H.M.S. *Stork*, seen off Chiswick in 1939. Built at Poplar in 1882 as a single-screw gunboat, she had a displacement tonnage of 465. Briefly used as a survey vessel she became a training ship in 1913 and was scrapped at Gillingham in 1950. Behind the trees on the right are some of London's reservoirs; Hammersmith Bridge is on the far left.

AND ON TO PUTNEY

Right: Annual highspot: Excursion craft leave Hammersmith Bridge astern as they follow the contestants in the 1948 University Boat Race. The haze over them is a reminder that two of the three vessels were still steam driven. The nearest one is the *Viscountess*, with the *Viscount* in the centre and the *Queen Elizabeth* beyond.

Left: Funnel up! A local veteran, the steam tug *Margaret* (1898/58) seen from Putney Bridge, bound up-stream for Brentford where she was owned by Clements Knowling & Co. Steel hulled and 70 ft long, she had been built at Greenwich and had the customary tall funnel of her day. For each bridge this had to be hauled down by wire, but once released it would be pulled upright by counter-weights. (1939)

Right: As the tide starts to ebb so the river tanker *Ben Sadler* (1931/289) approaches Putney Bridge, bound downstream after discharging at the National Benzole Co's depot just below Hammersmith Bridge. She was one of six - all with *Ben* names - then owned by the Company. (1939)

Above: The motor collier *Camroux III* (1931/409) passes Putney Embankment bound for the North East coast. She had come from the Rosebank Wharf, Fulham - about a mile upstream - which, like the vessel herself, was owned by the Newcastle Coal & Shipping Co. In later years this view would have been blocked by a new P.L.A. pier (1939)

Below: A scene on board the *P.L.A. Dredger No. 1* working off Putney in 1948. At regular intervals the dredger had to be winched to a slightly different position. As seen, a sextant - held horizontally - was used to check each new position against local landmarks. Such changes were then recorded on a chart.

Above: Used solely for the laying of moorings, Wm. Cory's *Cormooring* (1929/67) at work near Chelsea Bridge while one of Harrisons' tugs passes by with her funnel still only partly raised. Early post-war euphoria was such that the board over the *Cormooring*'s wheelhouse windows bore portraits of Churchill, Roosevelt and Stalin. (1946)

Below: In from the North East coast, the *Wimbledon* (1931/1,598) passes the Houses of Parliament (and the still war-scarred St. Margaret's Tower) carrying some 2,400 tons of coal for the Wandsworth gas works, whose annual intake was around 500,000 tons. Of all London's 'flatties' the Wandsworth ones were the pace-setters for size, even though they had the greatest distance to go up-river and had to negotiate nearly a score of bridges. (c.1946)

Left: A full-size replica of Henry Bell's *Comet* at London's Little Venice in 1963. The original, Britain's first passenger steamer and Europe's first practical steamship, made her first trip from Port Glasgow in August 1812. She lasted eight years before being wrecked. This replica, built in 1962, formed the centrepiece of Port Glasgow's celebrations to mark the 150th anniversary of the introduction of the steamship.

Below left: Now we come in peace! The Danish Viking ship *Hugin* has crossed the North Sea by oar and sail. She passes below Blackfriars Bridge towards Richmond.

Below: The spritsail barge *Sara* (1902/50 tons net) displays her winning flags as she lies close to one of the Festival of Britain's most remarkable features, the Skylon. (1951)

REJUVENATION

Right: The slim-hulled *Queen Elizabeth* (1924/91), for long one of London's best-known excursion ships, seen off Westminster Pier when she was still steam-driven. (1949)

Left: History maker: At the Festival of Britain the Royal Navy shows off its very first gas-turbine driven craft, the 52 ft long Harbour Launch No. *3964.* Her newly-fitted 130 hp Rover T8 gas-turbine - together with gearbox - weighed a mere 600 lbs. The diesel it replaced occupied three times as much space and weighed two and a half tons.

Right: The same *Queen Elizabeth* as appears at the top of the page after being remodelled and fitted with a Crossley diesel. Beyond are two special features of the Festival of Britain, the partly assembled Skylon and the Dome of Discovery. County Hall is on the right. (1951)

THE EMBANKMENT AREA

Upper left: The famous *Discovery* (1901/752) spent many years off the Embankment before being moved, first down-river and then in 1986, to Dundee where she had been built for the Royal Geographical Society. The first of her many voyages to the Antarctic was made under the command of Captain R F Scott. (1972)

Left: In the early 1970s the *Ferry Prince* (1939/70) was the last Thames excursion craft to be steam driven, but soon she too was converted to diesel. A former Portsmouth-Gosport ferry and very beamy, she measured 72 x 18 ft.

Below: The *Caledonia* (1934/624), a former Clyde excursion steamer, was converted by Bass Charrington into a very popular floating restaurant-cum-pub *Old Caledonia*. Opened in May 1972, she was lost by fire some ten years later. (1972)

ACTIVITY IN THE UPPER POOL

Left: The Upper Pool viewed c. 1938 from the Fresh Wharf end of London Bridge, the Customs House just showing between the Mediterranean trader *Adjutant* (1922/1,942) and the light hulled Swedish *Tilda*. Of the near 40 ships then owned by the General S.N.Co., the former - bought in 1924 as Denholm's *Myrtlepark* - remained one of the largest.

Right: Every weekday one of the *Batavier* ships, owned by Wm. H. Muller & Co. sailed between London and Rotterdam and vice versa. Numbered *I, II, III,* etc., they were of some 1,300/1,500 tons apiece and carried about 70 first and 50 second-class passengers. The Dutch eel boats (right) were then constant visitors to Billingsgate Market. (c. 1931)

Left: Dairy produce from Denmark and the Baltic was traditionally handled at the several wharves facing the Tower of London. Discharging at one of them is the United Baltic Co's *Baltrader* (1919/1,699). Other regulars belonged to the Danish DFDS or came from Russia or Poland. (1932)

THE POOL *Above:* Barely a year to go. The excursion ship *Queen of the Channel* (1935/1,162) starting on a day trip from the Upper Pool in May 1939. A 19 knot vessel able to carry over 1,400 passengers, she had been built by Dennys of Dumbarton for the New Medway Steam Packet Co. In May 1940 she was sunk by air attack while returning from Dunkirk with troops.

Below: The first Palestinian ship ever to visit London, the 19 knot *Kedmah* (1927/3,504), then about to start a new career in the Mediterranean. Owned by Harris & Dixon's Kedem Palestine Line, she later became Israel's first passenger ship. Built as the *Kedah*, she had been the famed flagship of the Straits S.S.Co. (1947)

THE POOL - NOW A RECEPTION POINT   *Above:* The Upper Pool, now the home of H.M.S. *Belfast*, is also the reception point for ships on official visits - which generally moor alongside the World War 2 cruiser. She is allowed to use the initials H.M.S. by courtesy only, since she is actually owned by the specially formed Belfast Trust. Moored outside the frigate is the Romanian sail training ship *Mircea*. (1975)

Below: The newly completed *Dana Regina* (1974 /11,966) arriving on a publicity visit. Built for the DFDS Harwich-Esbjerg service, she was then the largest North Sea ferry and also the largest passenger ship to have been built in Denmark. The turning point for ships of any size is at Hanover Hole, a mile or so downstream.

From Tower Bridge to the Barrier

Lower Pool, St. Katharine Dock, London Docks, Limehouse Reach, Surrey Commercial Docks, Deptford Buoys, Greenwich, West India and Millwall Docks, East India Dock, Blackwall, the Flood Barrier.

Above: Waiting to load: some spritsail barges moored at a tier above the entrance to the Royal Docks. On the right is Goldsmith's *Speranza* of 1889, while alongside - with a deeper transom - is Metcalf's 1902-built *J.B.W.* (1934)

Below Tower Bridge

Right: The Central Electricity Generating Board's 'flattie' (up-river collier) *Hackney* (1962/1,738) has lowered her mast and funnel for the last time this voyage as she passes under the Tower Bridge bound for the North East coast and another cargo. She is doing so at low water, but at other states of the tide there may be only the minimum of clearance. (1968)

Below: Situated just below the Tower Bridge, the St. Katharine Dock (opened in 1828) has become a marina and home for various historic vessels such as the *Challenge* (1931/212). Built for the Elliot Steam Tug Co., of Gravesend, she eventually became the last steam-driven, ship-handling tug on the Thames. On the left is the famous Dickens Inn, then in the process of being rebuilt on a new site. (1974)

THE OLDER, SMALLER DOCKS

Above: Berthed at the eastern end of the London Docks, the newly-built *Ulster Duchess* (1946/507) was then used on the London-Channel Islands trade. On the left P & A Campbell's paddle steamer *Cambria* is waiting for her post-war refit. (1946)

Left: The Finnish barque *Pamir* (1905/2,796) in Shadwell Basin. Then newly returned to her owner, Capt. Gustaf Erikson - who had bought her in 1921 for £4,000 - she spent the war years under New Zealand ownership. Beyond is St. Paul's, Shadwell, often referred to as the Church of the Sea Captains. (1946)

Below: The steam coaster *Crossbill* (1920/309) owned by R & W Paul Ltd., a leading firm of east coast millers, lies in the river with several barges. All are waiting to load grain from a tramp steamer newly arrived at Bellamy's Wharf, Rotherhithe. (1934)

DOWN TOWARDS GREENWICH

Right: The Wilson Line's *Albano* (1947/2,239) had left the Upper Pool for the Millwall Dock, there to load for Denmark. Her light grey hull denotes that she was one of the Company's so-called 'butter boats' which carried dairy produce - as distinct from their general cargo ships which had dark green topsides. (1948)

Centre: Gaselee tugs, distinguished by three red rings on a buff funnel, at their Limehouse Reach base. Gaselee & Son, an old-established firm primarily concerned with the handling of lighters, normally named their tugs after insects or reptiles. (1939)

Below: The S.S. *Forth* (1922/1,058) at the Carron Co's wharves, St. Katharine's Way. She and the *Carron* sailed twice weekly between London and Grangemouth. Primarily ironfounders, her owners were famed for their Carronade guns which were used at Waterloo and Trafalgar. By tradition each of their ships carried a cannon ball at the top of the mainmast. (1939)

The Surrey Commercial Docks

The Surrey Commercial Docks were the only ones to be situated on the south bank of the river and, since they represented an amalgam of many old-established enterprises, their layout was very complex. The largest element, the Greenland Dock, covered 22 acres and had been sited on one of London's oldest enclosed docks, the Howland, which had been built some 30 years after the Great Fire of London. Instead of having the usual array of warehouses, the Howland Dock had been surrounded by a screen of trees, specially planted to act as windbreaks for its 200 to 300-ton sailing ship customers.

The Howland Dock was later used by the Greenland whaling and fishing industries and, in the course of time, it became known as the Greenland Dock.

Above: the *Empire Yukon* (1921/7,651) in the Greenland Dock. Captured a few years before as the Italian *Duchessa D'Aosta*, she once had accommodation for 40 passengers but the top of her superstructure, which housed them, had now been removed. Later known as the *Petconnie* she was scrapped in 1952 as the *Liu O*. (1946)

An early and small upstream means of access to the river, known as the Surrey entrance, was closed in 1967. From then on all traffic had to use the 580 x 80 ft. Greenland Entrance Lock. An exception to this was the small South Dock, which retained its own entrance lock but this measured only 220 x 48 ft.

For the last 50 years of its existence the Greenland Dock catered mainly for ships from North America, its best known users being Cunard, Furness Withy and Canadian Pacific. The cargoes handled included perishables - which needed extensive cold storage facilities- grain, spruce and Oregon pine. But one must not overlook the cargoes brought in by the many smaller vessels from the Baltic. While the larger ships stopped at the Greenland Dock there were several cuts which led to smaller inner docks - the Canada, Quebec (the newest, opened in 1920), Albion and the long and narrow Russia Dock. In all these the emphasis was on timber, mainly from Scandinavia and Russia. Generally this was brought in small ships, often aged and possessors of most interesting histories.

The off-loaded timber - always manhandled - was stacked nearby in piles anything up to 30 ft. high or more - or else floated into long ponds to await collection. In their own sphere the importance of the Surrey Commercial Docks was without parallel. During the 1920s they handled about 20% of all Britain's timber imports. Stacked by the acre, this timber gave the whole area an aromatic and resinous scent which was uniquely attractive. The final ship to leave the Greenland Dock was the Russian *Kandalakshales*, which passed through on the 22nd December 1970. By March 1977 the Port of London Authority had sold the last remaining portion of the Surrey docks to Southwark Borough Council.

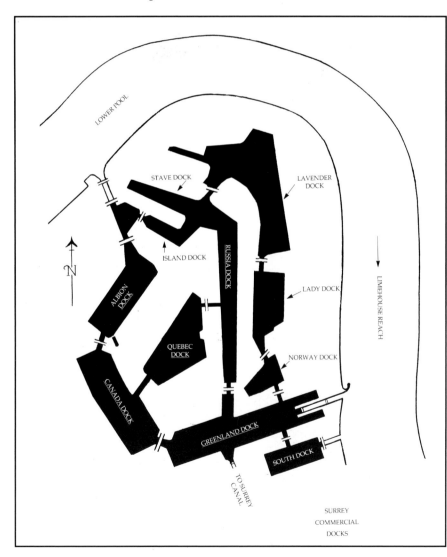

LOWER POOL

N

STAVE DOCK

LAVENDER DOCK

ISLAND DOCK

RUSSIA DOCK

ALBION DOCK

LADY DOCK

LIMEHOUSE REACH

QUEBEC DOCK

CANADA DOCK

NORWAY DOCK

GREENLAND DOCK

SOUTH DOCK

TO SURREY CANAL

SURREY COMMERCIAL DOCKS

Right: The Liberty ship *Newton D Baker* (1943/7,176) discharging at the river end of the Greenland Dock. In the foreground is the cut leading to the Norway Dock and through that to the 34-acre Lady and Lavender Timber Ponds. The *Newton D Baker*, then on charter to Lykes Bros., kept her name until she went to the breakers in 1968. (1947)

Below: The view from the dock entrance with the cranes of the West India Docks just visible on the far bank. On the left the General S.N. Co's *Oriole* (1939/489) is waiting to enter the lock, while the same Company's *Ptarmigan* (1948/959) passes downstream bound for the Continent.

Left: The Russia Dock, looking north east on a busy but quite typical day in October 1951. From left to right are the *Asturias* (1912/1,796), the grey-hulled *Savonia* (also Finnish) and a Swedish veteran, the 1,711-ton *Ulea* which was built in Newcastle in 1884 as the *CymroDorian*. Finally the bows of a new German ship are visible, the 2,459-ton *Gertrud Schliewen*. The large timber ponds lay some distance beyond the Finnish ships.

Centre: The *Trebol* (1902/2,668) - seen in the Canada Dock - was another veteran to come with timber. Built in Belgium as the *Princesse* (later *Reine*) *Elisabeth*, she was blown up by the Bolsheviks in 1918. Later the Estonian *Piret,* she served Ireland between 1942 and 1946 as the *Irish Alder.* After then trading as the Panamanian *Trebol*, she was scrapped at Blyth in 1952. (1946)

Below: Making her way towards the Greenland lock, the *Voosi* (1914/1,148) was unusual for her type in having been converted from steam to diesel in 1959. She measured 221 x 36 ft. and had been built as the Svea Line's *Skaraborg*. Sold to other Stockholm owners in 1954, her transfer to Costa Rican colours was an early example of Swedish flagging out. (1964)

Left: The strangely rigged *Werner Vinnen* (1922/1,859) in the Canada Dock during the 1930s. She was one of several German *Vinnen* sailers built at Kiel which were fitted with diesels originally intended for U-Boats. In 1937 she was rebuilt as a full-powered motorship.

Below right: Seen from the Station Yard (Canada Dock) and moored at the buoys, the Greek *Prenton* (1906/2,088) was then ready to discharge into lighters. Built at Glasgow as the *Ravelston*, she spent the war years as the *Empire Bond*. Sold Greek in 1946, she was wrecked three years later. (1947)

Above left: Work ceased at the weekends and then, especially on winter evenings, the whole dock area could become a misty, eerie void of silence. Lying at the Canada buoys is the dim form of the *Sherborne* and (left) that of the *Kingsborough*. In the foreground is the cut leading to the Albion Dock. (1947)

Right: Negotiating the cut from the Canada Dock to the Greenland, the Swedish *Hanna* (1917/ 2,624) was leaving a slight mantle of snow for grim conditions in the North Sea and beyond. Built for Cardiff owners as the *Firtree*, she became in turn the *Maindy Forest, Uskside, Agne* and then *Hanna*. (1955)

THE DEVELOPMENT OF TIMBER HANDLING

Some revolutions occur so gradually that it is only in retrospect that one can appreciate their full significance. So with the carriage and handling of timber. The old sailing ships - known as 'onkers' - which brought in Baltic timber gave way to newer auxiliary-powered schooners and handy sized steamers, often of considerable age. However, their low capital costs became offset by extravagant crew and fuel bills. The small diesel-driven 'paragraph' vessels which took their place scored in both directions but their cargoes were still stowed and handled in the traditional manner, almost plank by plank. The ocean-wide carriage of timber and forest products called for very much larger ships but the same problems applied. However, high capital costs demanded a quick turnaround and so led to pre-packaging and entirely new thinking in terms of deck equipment.

Above: Whatever the load, there was usually pleasure in being photographed, (Canada Dock, 1949)

Above right: The Swedish post-war auxilliary-powered schooner *Birgitta* (1945/229) in the Albion Dock in 1951. Steel hulled, she had a length of 113 ft.

Below: Once a common sight: the Estonian auxiliary schooner *Polarstjernen* (1918/337) with timber stowed on deck and below. Built of wood in Sweden, she was 135 ft long.

Right: The Swedish *Kalmarsund VIII* (1956/494) in the Albion Dock. when she was only a few months old. Her cargo of Baltic softwood is still being discharged in traditional style and at least 15 men are involved. The use of lighters added an extra stage to the sequence. (1956)

Right: The *Vasya Alekseev* (1967/4,677) with a deckload of Russian timber packaged and bound by steel bands. She relied on new-style derrick-cranes mounted on revolving bases.

Below: The *Pacific Lumberman* (1971/23,588 at her Tilbury berth with gantry arms extended. Originally Swedish-owned, she had been designed to carry palletised cars to the North Pacific coast and return with forest products such as sawn timber, plywood etc. (1981)

Left: A close-up as one of her giant gantries lowered some half-dozen packages of wood or pulp. Whatever the size of a gang, those actually needed to work each hatch were - one man in the hold, one to work the gantry, one to check the overside clearance and, finally, one to drive the forklift truck. (1981)

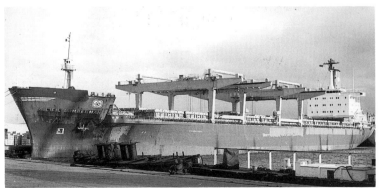

NEARING GREENWICH

Left: One of the most handsome prewar visitors to Greenwich Buoys was the *Monte Pascoal* (1930/13,870), photographed during one of those periods of relative peace on board when her passengers were ashore sightseeing. Owned by the Hamburg South American Line, she was one of a quartet built between 1924 and 1930, two of which came here periodically on cruises. (1935)

Left: The brand-new North Sea ferry *Winston Churchill* (1967/8,656) came to Greenwich to be officially christened by Lady Churchill. Instead of having to climb up the traditional steep and wobbly gangway, her guests entered by way of her stern door. This was easy but, once inside, the stairways leading up were too steep and narrow for crowds.

Left: Deptford Buoys, often used by large freighters, meant slow overside discharge into small craft. Waiting for her turn is a spritsail barge, identifiable as one of the steel-hulled Everard quartet built in 1925 and 1926. The four-master, the *Alster* (1928/8,514) was one of a group of ten owned by the North German Lloyd and, rather unusually, carried 16 passengers. Captured in 1940 and renamed *Empire Endurance*, she was torpedoed a year later. (1936)

Above: Marker buoys, etc. on the foredeck of the Post Office cable ship *Monarch* (1946/8,056). Like most British cable ships she was built on the Tyne by Swan, Hunter and Wigham Richardson. (1953)

Above: Seen loading cable, the *Recorder* (1954/3,349) then newly delivered to Cable & Wireless, was a slightly larger version of the *Edward Wilshaw* (1949) and *Stanley Angwin* (1952). On her first commission she took over the maintenance of cable in the area between Colombo and Vancouver.

Left: The *Dominia* (1926/9,273) then Britain's largest cable ship, was built to lay the long cable between British Columbia and the mid-Pacific Fanning Islands. For this work she sailed with 3,627 nautical miles of cable weighing 8,594 tons coiled in her four tanks. She was eventually made redundant and sold to Russia in 1937. (1932)

Left: The embellished stern of the *Cutty Sark* (1869/972), the only survivor of the tea clippers. Since 1954 she has been preserved in a specially prepared dry dock.

Above: The largest, most important users of Greenland Dock were five A-class Cunarders, built between 1921 and 1925 for the Canadian trade. *Alaunia* (1925/14,030) is in Gallions Reach and bound up-river. Turbine-driven and good for 15 knots, they were designed to carry some 500 cabin and 1,200 third class passengers. (1938)

Below: The Canadian Pacific *Beaverbrae* (1928/9,956) nearing the Greenland Dock where, in terms of size, she and her four sisters were second only to the Cunard A-class liners. These 520 ft long 14-knot turbine-driven ships burned pulverised coal - then a novelty. Amongst the finest cargo liners afloat when new, none survived the war. The only sizeable ships to go further up-river were either visitors to the Upper Pool or grain carriers bound for Bellamy's Wharf, Rotherhithe. (c.1938)

THE WEST INDIA DOCKS

The West India and East India Docks were opened in 1802 and 1806 respectively and thus pre-dated the arrival of the first steamship on the Thames - an event which did not occur until 1815. Each dock represented a different monopoly. The owners of the first one, who received much of their capital from the City's West India merchants, were granted a 21-year monopoly of all cargoes going to or coming from the West Indies.

The Honourable East India Company, long holders of a monopoly of all trade to and from India, the East Indies and China, soon followed with their own and much smaller dock. Once these monopolies had been abolished, competition between the two docks became so intense that in 1885 they were forced to amalgamate.

The West India Dock originally consisted of two parallel stretches of water, each 2,600 ft long, these being located at the top (north) end of the Isle of Dogs. Just to the south a ship canal was made to overcome the tedious passage round the loop of the river. A financial failure, it was widened and made into a third (and longer) part of the dock system and one, which in its early days, had projecting (north-south) jetties. To the east of these docks there were also the small Blackwall Basin, the Junction Dock and the railway-owned Poplar Dock.

The Millwall Dock, which was opened in 1864, originally had its own up-river entrance, but in the 1920s this was replaced by a newly-made cut which linked it with the West India group. For the latter, then being modernised, a new and larger entrance lock was built which measured 550 x 80 ft. This was later used to serve both dock systems. Over the period covered by this book these docks were mainly used by regular traders. The emphasis was on cargo, although passengers were also carried by the Union-Castle, Natal, Harrison and Swedish Lloyd lines and by the Aznar and larger Fred. Olsen ships which followed later.

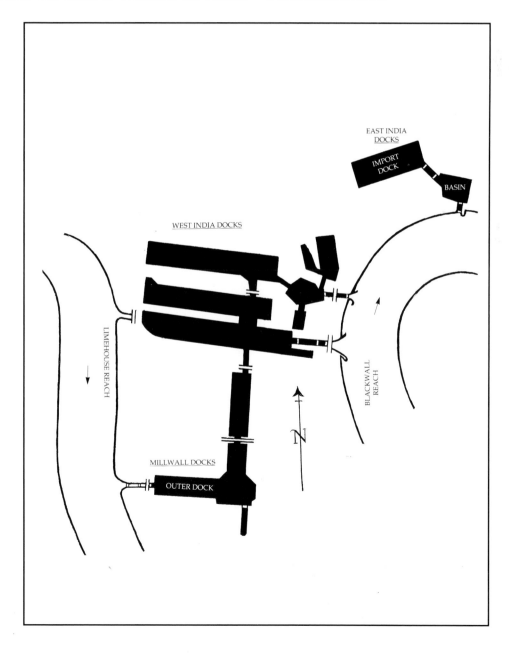

Left: The 16-knot *Riebeeck Castle* (1946/8,322) being coaxed into the West India entrance lock. A ship with over 420,000 cubic feet of insulated space, she and her sister *Rustenburg Castle* were the last Union-Castle reefers to be built at Belfast. The coaster seen end-on on the right was berthed approximately over the busy Blackwall Tunnel. (1966)

Left: The veteran tug *Vincia* (1909/150), one of Watkins' so-called 'Teddy Bear' class, leads the ex-German *Empire Tagralia* (1929/5,824) into the lock. This Swedish-built tanker, originally named *Max Albrecht* after her owner, was interned in Spain during the war. Surrendered and given her *Empire* name in 1945, she next became the *Repton* and subsequently the Italian *Alcantara*. (1945)

Above: The old West India Dock entrance - later modernised - with the Alexander tug *Sun VIII* (1919/198) assisting the *Ocean Wayfarer* (1942/7,178) to the river. (c.1946)

Left: Ellerman ships were constant users of the West India Docks. The *City of Hull* (1947/8,459) was one of a 16-knot quartet and served the company for 20 years before finally going to Japanese breakers as the Panamanian registered *Essex.* (1956)

Below: Unusual visitor: H.M.S. *Finnwhale*, one of the 295 ft-long *Porpoise* class submarines, has cleared the lock and makes for her berth just ahead. On the left, and distinguished by the wide top of her Velle mast, is the Harrison Line's *Philosopher.*

33

A CENTURY OF STEMS

Above left: The graceful stem of the laid-up *Triton*, once a tender to the Gravesend Sea School. Soon after, the figurehead vanished by accident or design. (c.1950)

Above right: The beautiful bronze and painted figurehead of the Norwegian *Bencomo* (1950/2,937), one of the Fred. Olsen Line's U.K. - Canary Islands traders. The Company's use of figureheads - which won worldwide fame - started in 1936 following the adoption of rounded as compared to knife-pointed stems. (1957)

Left: Relic of the steam and sail era: H.M.Coal Hulk *C.109* (1865/10,500t. displacement) shortly before being broken up in 1950. In her heyday she was the 400 ft cruiser H.M.S. *Agincourt* with two funnels and five canvassed masts, the longest ship in the Royal Navy.

Below: The *Empire Ridley* (1941/6,838), a standard ship used from 1943 as H.M.Cable Ship *Latimer* to help lay the Pluto pipelines across the Channel, these to keep our advancing forces supplied with fuel - hence the bow sheaves. She was sold in 1947 to become the Italian *Acheo*. Her days ended in a Japanese breaker's yard in 1964. (1946)

FRUIT, PASSENGERS AND GENERAL CARGO   *Above:* The Norwegian fruit ship *Bengazi* (1947/ 2,193) outward bound from the Canary Wharf, has negotiated the double-bend and heads for the lock. A 15-knot vessel of 3,800 tons dead weight, she was the first post-war addition made to Fred. Olsen's Mediterranean fleet. To the left is the Harrison Liberty ship *Statesman* and, beyond, an Ellerman vessel. (1949)

Below: The stately *Llanstephan Castle* (1914/11,293) which, with her sister *Llandovery Castle* (sunk during World War I) were the first Union-Castle ships to be built for the new Philipps/Kylsant regime and, as such, introduced a more lofty profile to the fleet. A two-class, 14-knot ship designed for service to East Africa, she lasted until 1952.

Above: The 21-knot cargo liner *Bencruachan* (1968/12,092) which had broken her back after hitting a freak wave when off the East African coast. In South Africa she was stiffened, patched and given temporary repairs to enable her to reach the U.K. After discharging she went on to Rotterdam where the final work was carried out. Not long afterwards a brand-new container ship - still on her maiden voyage - was in that same area when she encountered a similar giant wave which completely broke off her bows. (1973)

Below: The 15-knot S.S. *Jamaica Producer* (1934/5,464) was the only one of the Jamaica banana fleet to survive the war. Attacked by a German bomber, she instead shot it down, and so, for some years, her funnel carried a small painted representation of her downed assailant. Scrapped in 1962, her name was given to a new and faster motor vessel. (c.1948)

WEST INDIA AND MILLWALL DOCKS

Above: A Russian-built Raketa hydrofoil in for repairs at Millwall. So far all efforts to run a successful hydrofoil service down-river have failed. This craft, which operated from near Tower Bridge, was leased, but the option of purchase was not pursued. Floating debris and damaged foils aggravated poor time-keeping. (c.1975)

Below: The Cunard Line's *Scotia* (1966/5,825) berthed near the swing bridge which spanned the West India-Millwall cut. A seventeen and a half knot vessel of 7,450 tdw, she was the newest of a seven-ship series - all with engines aft - to be built for the North Atlantic service. She was sold in 1970 and became the *Neptune Amber*.

Above: In from Gothenburg, the Svenska Lloyd *Saga* (1946/6,647) makes for her Millwall berth. Her first sailing from London in 1946 will long be remembered by the author who, like countless others, had become hardened to the austerities of wartime rationing. What she offered her passengers seemed like food from another world! After operating with the *Suecia* and *Britannia*, she was sold to become the *Ville de Bordeaux* and then the Bulgarian *Nessebar*. (1956)

Below: As the spritsail barge *Kathleen* (1901/60 net) loads grain from one of the spouts at Millwall her almost full hold needs constant trimming by hand. The arrangement of hatch beams, covers and heavy canvas outer layer are traditional.

MILLWALL DOCK

Right: Strick Line ships were amongst the best known and frequent users of the Millwall and West India Docks. Two are shown at their usual berths opposite the Millwall grain jetty. The nearer one, the *Baluchistan* (1956/5,950) was then the company's largest and their first to exceed 500 ft. Like the great majority of this fleet, she had been built by Readhead's yard at South Shields. (1956)

Centre: The *Lazar Kaganovich* (1937/11,000 tons displacement) at Millwall for major overhaul. This lasted about two years and it was August 1949 before she finally left for Murmansk. One officer, who thought little of British labour, said that at home such slowness would have warranted a firing squad! One of a class of four ice-breakers which were then Russia's largest and most powerful, she measured 350 x 75.5 ft, had triple screws and a combination of both steam and diesel-electric machinery, the latter being used at cruising speeds. (1949)

Below: The Prince Line's Mediterranean traders which had long used the West India Docks later moved to Millwall. This coincided with a company policy change to chartering smaller vessels. *Celtic Prince* (1967/1,439) was typical. This name lasted from 1968 to 1977 when she reverted to *Arbon*. Dutch owned, she flew the attractive and rarely seen Netherlands Antilles flag. (1969)

EAST INDIA DOCK

Of London's older docks, the East India was the furthest downstream. It was also small and, even with its entrance basin, it only occupied 31 acres of water. Amongst the last of the many passenger ships to go there were the *Empire Parkeston* and the *Kelantan*.

Upper: The North Sea troopship *Empire Parkeston* (1930/5,556), seen undergoing refit, was then managed by General Steam and used to carry BAOR (British Army of the Rhine) personnel, mainly between Harwich and the Hook of Holland. Built as the three-funnelled *Prince Henry*, she was first used by Canadian National Steamships along the west coast of Canada but, during the war, she saw service first as an AMC (Armed Merchant Cruiser) and then as an LSI (Landing Ship, Infantry). (1948)

Lower: The Far Eastern passenger ship *Kelantan* (1921/1,665) of the Straits Steamship Co. leaving for her home port, Singapore, in November 1947, after six years of Naval service had been made good. A ship of remarkably shallow draught, she drew only ten feet of water. Towing her is J.P. Knight's *Khurdah* (1930/50), one of the earlier of the local tugs to be diesel-driven.

FROM BLACKWALL REACH TO WOOLWICH REACH

Upper left: A sight once too familiar to warrant attention. One of the many Cory tugs, the steam-driven *Reserve* (1934/32), proceeds downstream towing six lighters - the maximum permitted on the river. Beyond her lies the entrance to the London Docks while under the river bed is the Rotherhithe Tunnel. (1948)

Upper right: Owner inspects damage. The steam coaster *Copthall* (1922/973) had just berthed at Mast Pond Wharf, Woolwich, after colliding with the Elder Dempster ship *Ebani*. *Copthall* was her fourth name - she started life as the Newcastle-registered *Emilie Dunford*. (1957)

Centre left: The American standard ship *Sarcoxie* (1919/5,116) bound for West India Docks. The design lacked sheer, camber and good looks, but proved to be amongst the most successful U.S. war-built types. A turbine-driven ship of 7,500 tdw, she became the *Alcoa Ranger* in 1940, two years before she was sunk (1939)

Left: Buoys of all shapes and sizes stored at Corporation of Trinity House depot at Blackwall. The ship, still in wartime paint, is the Falkland Islands' *Discovery II* (1929/1,036) in use by Trinity House. (1949)

BLACKWALL FLOODING - BEFORE THE BARRIER

Left: The floods of March 1949 affected two ships which were under repair in the Blackwall dry docks. The *William H Daniels* (1923/1,772) had some of her bottom plates off, so promptly filled as the tide poured over the dock sill. Then being made ready for her return to Canada, she was typical of so many 'Canallers' brought over for wartime use as North Sea colliers but which, in winter, proved quite unsuitable owing to their low power and general unhandiness.

Centre: In the adjacent dock Coast Lines' *Eastern Coast* (1922/1,223) was lifted off her blocks, eventually settling with a heavy list. The Blackwall yard was centuries old, for one of the early warships built there was the 62-gun H.M.S. *Dreadnought* of 1653.

Below: The Thames Barrier, which brought belated protection to the City of London, was officially opened by the Queen and Prince Philip in May 1984. To achieve similar down-river safety many miles of anti-flood walls had to be built which, by their construction, swept away many historic features.

THE FREE FERRY

The Woolwich Ferry which links the north and south shores has been a free one since March 1887 when the present service was opened by Lord Rosebery, Chairman of the then new London County Council. However, Woolwich has had a ferry for many centuries - since it was a small fishing village. The earliest known reference is in a document dated 1308, which records it as having changed hands for £10. The switch from paddle to Voith Schneider propulsion came in 1963 when the fleet was reduced from four to three.

Above and right: The *Will Crooks* and *John Benn* (both 1930/621) joined an earlier pair, the *Squires* and *Gordon* of 1922 and 1923. Sisters, all were built at East Cowes, measured 166 x 44 ft, carried 1,000 passengers and up to 100 tons of vehicles. Each paddle had its separate single-condensing engine, while the two boilers used coke at 50 lbs (40 for the first pair) which came from the local gas works.

Below: Seen from the top of an office block, the *John Burns* (foreground) is approaching the south shore, while *Ernest Bevin* nears the northern terminal. These two and the *James Newman* (all 1963/738) comprise the present fleet. Compared with the previous ones, they carry 200 tons of vehicles but only some 500 passengers. Built at Dundee, they measure 185 x 63 ft and have two diesel-driven Voith Schneider units, one at each end. (1978)

From Woolwich to Northfleet

The Royal Docks (Royal Victoria, Royal Albert, and King George V), Gallions Reach, Erith, Purfleet, Greenhithe, St. Clement's Reach, West Thurrock, Grays, Northfleet Grain Terminal.

The 14-knot *Beaverpine* (1962/4,390) was one of the third generation of Canadian Pacific *Beaver* ships. Much smaller than those of the 1928 and 1946 series, they were designed to use the new Canadian Seaway route to the Great Lakes.

THE ROYAL DOCKS

The Royal Docks comprised three separate units, the Royal Victoria Dock, the Royal Albert (and its associated basin) and the King George V. The oldest of these, the Victoria, was officially opened in 1855 but did not receive its Royal prefix until 1880 when the Duke of Connaught opened the second one, the Royal Albert. An even longer period - over 40 years - elapsed before the last of the three was declared open by King George V in 1921.

The Victoria, which was designed to handle worldwide trade, originally had 25.5 ft. of water and eight projecting jetties. Its 94 acres of water were served by an up-river entrance lock which measured 325 x 80 ft. It was the first dock to be linked with the main railway system and also the first to use hydraulic power for its machinery. Its purchase early-on by the London & St. Katharine's Dock Co. led to the development of earlier expansionist plans - which culminated in the construction of the Royal Albert Dock.

This catered for larger ships, had 27 ft. depth of water and was the first to use electric lighting. At its down-river end it had a basin and an entrance lock which measured 550 x 80 ft. It also had two dry docks, these 500 and 575 ft. long, which were located at the opposite end - near the Connaught cut, which led through into the Royal Victoria. As far back as 1889 the latter had pioneered the handling of meat cargoes, this being followed in 1902 by the construction of several silos, after which the Royal Victoria became the venue for very many grain ships. The creation of the Port of London Authority in 1908 brought an end to the private ownership of London's docks and, with it, old rivalries. Much expansion followed, including - in 1910 - extra facilities for the handling of frozen and chilled meat, a trade in which the Royal Albert dock became involved.

The completion of the King George V dock in 1921 added another 64 acres of water to the Royals and raised the total to approximately 245 acres. A special feature here was the provision of seven dolphins, each 520 ft. long which were placed 32 ft. away from the quay. Ships berthed there could thus discharge either side into lighters or, alternatively, on to the quay and its rail system. The King George V, which had a 750 ft. long dry dock at its western end, was linked to the other docks by a 100 ft. wide channel. This was located near the new entrance lock which measured 800 x 100 ft. and had 45 ft. of water.

Together the Royal docks handled a wide variety of cargoes, notably tobacco, dairy produce and meat. Of the many famous lines which they served, most traded either to the Americas, the Far East or Australasia. The development of new trades, the advent of containerisation and the fact that Tilbury was many miles nearer the sea led inevitably to the run-down of these long-famous docks. The first closure, that of the Royal Victoria, came in 1983 and by two years later the last ship laid up in the King George V dock had left.

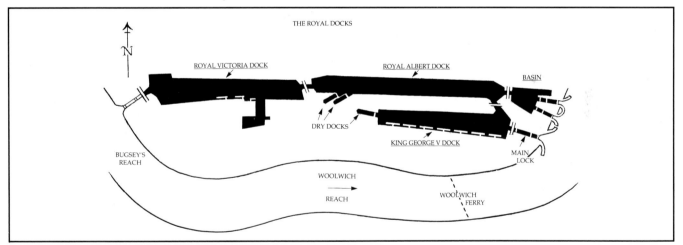

THE ROYAL DOCKS

ROYAL VICTORIA DOCK

ROYAL ALBERT DOCK

BASIN

DRY DOCKS

KING GEORGE V DOCK

MAIN LOCK

BUGSEY'S REACH

WOOLWICH

REACH

WOOLWICH FERRY

N

Right: The great length of the Royal Albert dock as seen from the U.S. Lines' brand-new *American Challenger* as she approached her berth in the Royal Victoria dock at the end of her maiden voyage. Also important as being the first of a series, she was given a siren greeting from the ships she passed, the last in the row being the British India liner *Nardana* (1956/8,511) seen on the right. (1962)

ENTRANCE TO THE ROYALS

Left: The 14-knot turbine-driven *Achilles* (1920/11,246) was one of the later and larger Blue Funnel ships to have goal-post masts. From 1940 to 1948 she served as the Naval depot ship *Blenheim*. (c.1937)

Below: The Watkins tug *Napia* makes for the King George V dock, where the *Ocean Cock* is handling a Port liner. Access to the other Royal docks was provided by a cut (not visible) on the right. (1958)

Above: The 16-knot *City of Baltimore* (1919/8,424) was one of five used between 1931 and 1938 on the Baltimore Mail Line's service from Baltimore to London and the Continent. Former transports, each carried 80 tourist class. Subsequent use by the Panama Pacific Line ended with the war. (c.1937)

Below: Coming to a later generation, the 17-knot *Pando Gulf* (1957/8,753) was one of seven P & O ex-British India ships which were given *Pando* names and operated to the Far East. The former *Woodarra*, she was scrapped as the *Benalbanach* in 1978. (1970)

PRE-WAR DAYS IN THE ROYAL ALBERT DOCK

Right: The P & O Line's *Mantua* (1909/ 10,946) was one of the famous 'M' class of which ten were built between 1903 and 1912. A 16-knot vessel, she carried some 400 first and 200 second class passengers. She was mainly used on the Australian trade. The last of her class to remain in service, she was broken up in Shanghai in 1935. (1932)

Left: The ever-popular Port of London Authority dock cruises provided a good way of seeing something of London's shipping. Here, in the Royal Albert Dock, the *Ruahine* (1909/ 10,832) is berthed ahead of the Shaw Savill Line's *Mamari* and *Mahana*. The *Ruahine*, built by Denny, served the New Zealand Line for 40 years - longer than any other ship - and then spent another eight as the Grimaldi Line's *Auriga* before being scrapped in Genoa. (1932)

Right: Another long-lasting favourite on the New Zealand run was the *Ionic* (1902/ 12,352). Together with her sisters *Athenic* and *Corinthic* she was built for the White Star-Shaw Savill joint service. Designed to carry some 370 passengers in three classes, these were later cut to two and then, subsequently, confined to tourist class. She went to Japanese breakers in 1936. (1932)

THE ROYAL ALBERT DOCK - POST-WAR

Below left: Period styles for bow and stern seen in the Royal Albert. The former is that of the British India Company's *Itinda*, a cargo liner of 1938 vintage. The cruiser stern is that of the rather larger - 8,071 ton - Brocklebank liner *Macharda* which was also built that year. (1955)

Upper right: The Union-Castle Line's *Pretoria Castle* (1939/17,392) in the Royal Albert Dock at the end of her maiden voyage. During the war she was used first as an Armed Merchant Cruiser and then rebuilt as an Escort Carrier (Training). Bought back by Union-Castle, she was rebuilt between 1946 and 1947 and then re-commissioned as the *Warwick Castle* and, as such, lasted until 1962. In the foreground is the Alexander tug *Sun II* (1909/197)

Lower right: The passenger and cargo liner *Aragon* (1960/18,575) at her regular Z- shed berth at the top end of the Victoria Dock. She and her sisters *Amazon* and *Arlanza* were the last of their type to be built for Royal Mail Lines - who sold them to Shaw Savill in 1968. She then became the *Aranda* but was later converted into a Norwegian car carrier. (c. 1962)

REMINDERS OF WAR

Left: Still afloat even if war-stained, the Glen Line's *Glenaffaric* (1920/7,782) at her home dock - the King George V - in 1946. Originally the *Machaon*, and the first of a quartet built in Scotland for the Blue Funnel Line, she alone survived the war. She was finally scrapped at Briton Ferry in 1951. (1946)

Below right: The knifelike bows of Blue Star Line's *Brisbane Star* (1937/12,791) temporarily repaired after a torpedo had destroyed the lower part during a Malta convoy. She was one of those which were familiarly known as 'Empire Food Ships' because of their high speed and large reefer capacitty. (1947)

Above left: Details of the Liberty steamer *Samjack* (1944/7,210) in the Victoria Dock in 1946. Both the AA gun pods on her bridge are empty but she still retained her emergency rafts since mines were still a hazard. Her wartime livery is broken by a new feature - a narrow blue band on the funnel signifying Blue Funnel management.

Right: Already in her peacetime livery, the fast Victory type steamer *St Lawrence Victory* (1945/7,607) in the Royal Albert Dock in 1946. A then novel American custom, which initially caused some amusement, was that of having the ship's name preceded by the letters S.S.

ACCENT ON GRAIN

Left: The Cardiff-owned tramp *Madras City* (1940/5,052) which has just discharged her cargo of grain is being towed down the Victoria Dock by the *Sun X* (1920/196) A ship of pre-Empire design, the *Madras City* was built at Haverton Hill for the Reardon Smith Line. Kept for 18 years, she then became the *Chittagong City* before going to Karachi breakers three years later. (1956)

Left: A Port of London Authority grain elevator bound for the Victoria Dock being towed through the Royal Albert. Grain sucked from a vessel's hold was discharged into lighters moored alongside - or else into small coasters.

Below: It was with this ship, the *Indian Enterprise* (1946/7,319), that the India Steamship Company inaugurated their Calcutta - London service in 1950. Later that year she was bound from the Continent and London for Calcutta with a cargo which included 580 tons of explosives when she blew up and sank with the loss of all but one of her crew. Sunderland built, she had started her career as the *Empire Mombasa*. (1950)

REEFERS ALL

Above: For Port Line ships streamlining did not appear until well after World War 2, one of the best looking being *Port Launceston* (1957/10,285). Built in Belfast for the Australasian trade, she carried only ten passengers and had considerable insulated storage space. Sold in 1977, she then became the *United Vantage*. (1958)

Left: History carried on her bows: The owners of the *Port Nelson* were formed in 1914 through the merger of four companies - Corry, Milburn, Royden and Tyser. Port names were inherited from Milburn, the double-cross flag from Tyser. Red funnels followed purchase by Cunard in 1916.

Below: Elders & Fyffes' turbo-electric *Sinaloa* (1932/7,513) after she had been converted to cargo only and her profile mutilated by the removal of the after part of her superstructure. When built as the *Veragua* for the United Fruit Company's Caribbean trade she carried 95 passengers. (1960)

AUSTRALASIAN TRADERS

Above: The white-painted *Gothic* (1948/15,911) of the Shaw Savill Line ready for her 1953 Royal Tour of Australia and New Zealand. She was one of a 17-knot, 85-passenger quartet, her earlier sisters being the *Corinthic*, *Athenic* and *Ceramic*. When sold to Taiwan breakers in 1969 she was still carrying the scars of an earlier fire.

Left: Meat from Aberdeen & Commonwealth Line's *Largs Bay* (1921/14,182) being transferred to a cold store in the Royal Albert Dock. The ship was one of five *Bays* built for the state-controlled Commonwealth Government Line, but constant labour troubles led to their early sale - after which conditions improved. (1947)

Right: The ever-popular *Akaroa* (1914/15,130), a 15-knot Shaw Savill ship which was built in Belfast as the Aberdeen Line's *Euripides*. She was bought in 1932, renamed and converted to oilfuel. She was also fitted out to carry around 200 passengers. After an outstandingly successful career she was sold in 1954 to Belgian breakers. (c.1938)

FUNNEL CONTRASTS - INDICATIONS OF AGE

Above: The British India Line's *Durenda* (1922/7,241) was the Company's first cargo ship of any size to be diesel driven. She was the second of a 450 ft trio, the others being the passenger carrying *Domala* and *Dumana*. Twin screw ships, they were propelled by North British diesels of 3,750 bhp. Despite bomb damage in 1941 the *Durenda* was kept until 1958. (1946)

Centre: The 17-knot *Yasukuni Maru* (1930/11,933) and *Terukuni Maru* were the first motorliners to be put on the Nippon Yusen Kaisha's old-established mail service from Japan to London. This was brought to a close in November 1939 when the *Terukuni Maru* was sunk by magnetic mine near Ramsgate. (1938)

Left: The British India *Uganda* (1953/14,430) seen just before her maiden voyage was designed to carry 300 passengers, first and tourist. Although her 1967-8 conversion into a schools cruise ship spoiled her original good looks, it did extend her life. Later she became famous as a hospital ship in the Falklands War. She ended her days in the hands of Taiwan breakers.

FOR PILGRIMS, BANANAS AND PASSENGERS

Right: The newly-delivered pilgrim ship *Mozaffari* (1948/7,024) preparing for her maiden voyage. She and the *Mohammedi* were built for the Mogul Line's India - Jeddah service and had accommodation for 62 first and 1,399 deck class passengers. Reciprocating machinery and an exhaust turbine gave a speed of 14.5 knots.

Centre: The yacht-like Norwegian reefer *North Star* (1948/3,870) discharging bananas in the Royal Albert Dock. An 18-knot vessel she had accommodation for 12 passengers. Like the *Northern Lights* - also owned by Chr Haaland of Haugesund - she was on long-term charter to the Jamaica Banana Producers' Association, hence her blue and white funnel markings. (1947)

Below: The handsome *City of Durban* (1954/13,345) and her sisters (named after *Exeter, Port Elizabeth* and *York*) carried just over 100 first class passengers and were designed for the Ellerman & Bucknall Line's monthly service to South and East Africa. Built on the Tyne by Vickers-Armstrongs, their Doxford diesels gave a speed of 16.5 knots. Sold to Karageorgis in 1971, two of them were later rebuilt as Adriatic ferries. (1956)

BUSTLE IN THE ROYAL ALBERT

Left: Seen on a busy day, the Shaw Savill Line's *Britannic* (1962/12,228) is just one of a long row in the Royal Albert Dock with (right) an example of venerable old age - the spritsail barge *Cambria* (1906/79 net). The *Britannic*, like her sister *Majestic*, carried her Stulcken heavy derrick in upright position and, to avoid a blind spot, had her radar scanner set extra high. (1969)

Centre: The outward bound *Fremantle Star* (1944/9,883) was one of the standard 15-knot Empire series and, over 25 years, bore six different names. Towing her is the twin-screw *Platina* (1952/159) which, like the *Plagal*, *Plangent* and *Plateau*, had been built by Scarr's of Hessle. (1957)

Below left: The Port of London Authority tug *Plankton* (1965/122) handling a new arrival. She was one of a Dunston-built quartet and, like the *Placard*, *Plasma* and *Platoon*, relied on Voith-Schneider propulsion. Beyond her is the 21-knot cargo liner *Benalbanach*. (1970)

Below right: From 1926 onwards this strange-looking ferry provided a link between the two sides of the Royal Albert Dock. She was both propelled and steered by a Gill water-jet which could be swung through 360 degrees. (1956)

EXIT FROM THE ROYALS

The entrance to the Royal Docks provided a fine view of river traffic as it passed along Gallions Reach with impressive close-ups of the ships bound to or from the docks themselves.

Right: The Cunard liner *Mauretania* (1939/39,655) backing out of the King George V Dock at the start of her maiden voyage. The largest passenger liner ever to use the dock, she measured 772x89ft.

Centre: The United States Lines' *American Reporter* (1945/8,287) swinging off the lock entrance before starting a voyage to the 'States. A 15-knot turbine ship, she was one of the numerous and very successful U.S.-built C-2 types, of which the United States Lines then owned 40. (1949)

Below: The Cunard Line's *Ivernia* (1955/21,717) being handled by the *Sun X* (foreground) and the *Sun XVIII* as she leaves for Canada. In 1962 she was converted into the cruise ship *Franconia* and, when sold in 1973, became the Russian *Fedor Shalyapin*. (1957)

CURTAINS DOWN *Above:* By 1982 the King George V Dock had become merely a convenient place in which to lay up. The upper end is seen across the bows of the bulk carrier *King Charles*. Behind the centre ship - the Greek *Ion* - is her twin, the *Iason*, and astern, the *Ephestos*.
Below: Like symbolic closing curtains, the sterns of the *King Charles* and *King Alfred* screen the Lyras-owned *Ion* (1971/11,250). The final exodus took place in 1985.

COLLIERS ALL

Right: Slightly downstream, Cory's Albert Dock Jetty received a constant stream of colliers bringing supplies for nearby Beckton Gas Works. Just in from the North East coast, the *Corbridge* (1928/1,703) is about to berth, while the *Arnewood* (beyond) is ready to leave. (1946)

Centre: A Stephenson Clarke ship, the *Rogate* (1946/2,849) discharging coal at Wm. Cory's then newly-modernised Erith Jetty - which is now a ro-ro (roll-on, roll-off) terminal. Originally known as the *Empire Gower*, the *Rogate* was sold in 1964, her name being repeated three years later. (1946)

Below: The *Betty Hindley* (1943/1,771) - the second so named - and *Cormead* at the Erith collier tier as they wait their turn to discharge. The *Betty Hindley* was unfortunately named since her namesake of 1941 lasted only a month before being wrecked, while she herself was sunk by a mine when only four years old. (1947)

OFF CRAYFORD NESS

Left: The veteran Finnish steamer *Elsa S* (1900/2,242) bound for the Surrey Commercial Docks with Baltic softwood. Then bearing her sixth name and almost at the end of her career, she had been built at Elsinore as the Russian *Katie*. (1955)

Centre: Another ship of many names, the 17-knot *Iberia Star* (1950/10,868) at the start of her first voyage to the River Plate. Built as the Congo liner *Baudouinville* (later *Thysville*), she next became the Booth Line's *Anselm* and for two years traded to the Amazon. After a similar period with Blue Star she was transferred to the Austasia Line and renamed *Australasia*. (1961)

Below: Traffic regulations ignored during the weekend rush: Passing four abreast round Crayfordness are the German (Argo Lines') 721 ton *Butt*, the 570-ton *Tynecastle*, the Dutch *Surte* (291 tons) and the Polish 486-ton *Nysa*. (c. 1952)

AROUND PURFLEET

Above: The ship unique, the Vlasov-owned *Fairsky* (1937/3,551) moored off Purfleet. Built at Kiel as the *Friesenland*, she was designed as a floating seadrome and used in pre-war years as a mid-ocean stopping point for the Dornier flying boats used by Lufthansa on its Germany - South America service. Lifted aboard by crane, they were serviced, refuelled and then catapulted off from a long runway aft. (1957)

Below: In Long Reach, as seen from the Watkins tug *Badia*, the British India Line's *Chilka* (1950/7,087) approaches the *Rhodesia Castle* (1951/17,041), then outward bound for East Africa. The latter was scrapped in 1967, but one sister, the *Kenya Castle*, later became well known as the Chandris cruise ship *Amerikanis*. (1956)

GREENHITHE

Above: Greenhithe waterfront, with the *Worcester* just visible on the left. Next come the College grounds, with the top of Ingress Abbey just visible. The Causeway (centre) - also shown below - is at the downstream end of the village. The Everard offices and wharf are to the right. Further on, but not shown, were the many oil tanks which were removed in 1981. (1962)

Upper right: The steam-driven *Agility* (1924/522) which, when new, was the largest in the Everard coaster fleet. She was also the first tanker to be built for the firm and their first to be ordered from a shipyard away from the Thames. (1935)

Lower right: The *Sincerity* (1971/1,596) moored off the local causeway - which marked the start and end of many a voyage. Everards were one of the several Thames-side firms to adopt variations of the corn-coloured hull first introduced by the Orient Line. (1978)

Below: High and dry for overhaul, the Tilbury-Gravesend ferry *Edith* (1961/214) reveals the three blades of her Voith-Schneider propulsion unit, one of which is end-on to the camera. (c.1985)

THE TWO WORCESTERS

Above: The *Worcester (II),* which lay off Greenhithe from 1877 to to the outbreak of World War II was laid down in 1833 as a 110-gun First Rate ship but after her launch in 1860 was fitted with auxiliary steam propulsion. As H.M.S. *Frederick William,* a 74-gun ship of 4,725 tons, she saw only the minimum of service. Loaned to the Thames Nautical Training College in 1876, she was stripped of her machinery and given the name of an earlier ship - a frigate - to receive her first cadets in February 1877. (c.1935)

Right: The same *Worcester* seen when anchored off Grays in 1947, two years after she had been returned to the Admiralty. Sold a year later to local breakers, she sank at her moorings. She was eventually raised and broken up in 1953.

*Above:*The slim and the portly - the *Cutty Sark* (1869/965) and the third *Worcester* (1904/5,480), the one designed as a clipper and the other for a purely static role. The former, previously moored at Falmouth, made her final sea passage in 1938 when she was towed to Greenhithe by the Watkins' tug *Muria*.Her final move to Greenwich took place in December in 1954. (1952)

Below: The *Worcester* up for sale with her galley chimney enlivened by graffiti in the form of an Esso logo. Beyond are the colliers *Battersea* and *Harry Richardson* (1951-50/both 1,777) then the last of the Thames 'flatties'. (1978)

UNDER WAY

Above: The Argentinian *Presidente Peron* (1949/ 12,549), one of a 19-knot trio built for the Dodero Line's London-Buenos Aires service. She carried 74 first class and made the passage in 16 days. After the 1951 fall of the Peronist Government she was renamed *Argentina*, her sisters *Eva Peron* and *17 de Octubre* becoming the *Uruguay* and *Libertad*. (1955)

Right: The spritsail barge *Joy* (56 tons net) glides gently downstream in 1951. Then owned at Rocheford, Essex by A.M. & H. Rankin Ltd of Stambridge Mills, she was built in 1914 by one of the creeks running into the River Swale.

Below: The outgoing Shaw Savill liner *Dominion Monarch* (1939/27,155) rounds Crayford Ness in 1958. The largest regular user of the Royal Docks, she was one of the world's largest motor liners, carrying 500 first class passengers at up to 21.5 knots. After use as a hotel ship for the Seattle World's Fair in 1962 she was sold for scrap. Her final voyage was as the *Dominion Monarch Maru*.

ST. CLEMENT'S REACH   *Above:* H.M.S. *Belfast*, as a 'dead ship', is towed up St. Clement's Reach in 1982, bound for her traditional berth near the Tower of London. She came from dry dock in Tilbury where she was last seen in 1971. Years earlier, in 1939, she was near Iceland when she made the largest capture of the war, the German liner *Cap Norte* (1922/13,615) which was later used as the *Empire Trooper*.

Below: The *Corchester* (1965/4,840) discharging at West Thurrock Power Station. One of a handsome Blyth-built trio she, like the *Pulborough* and *Rogate*, carried 7,000 tons of coal. The CEGB renamed her *Dolphin Point* in 1976.

GRAYS AND JUST BELOW

Right: Shipbreaking at Grays. The paddle steamer *Premier* (1846/129) awaiting demolition in T.W. Ward's yard. Previously owned by Cosens of Weymouth, she had been the world's oldest seagoing passenger ship. Beyond lie the remains of the *Dan* (1912/4,874) the first British-built ocean-going motorship. As the *Jutlandia*, she had been built for the East Asiatic Co. of Copenhagen. (1937)

Centre: The half-demolished tanker *San Adolfo* (1935/7,385) at Grays. She was one of the six-ship 'A' class which were the first motor tankers to be owned by Eagle Oil. Beyond, and waiting her turn, is H.M.S. *Welfare*, a World War 2 *Algerine*-class minesweeper. (1957)

Below: Inward bound from Belgium, the P & O *Jetfoil No 2* passes the Tilbury Grain Terminal which has the Houlder Line's *Ripon Grange* (1968/28,880) alongside. Then the Company's largest, this red-hulled bulk carrier was sold soon afterwards to become the Greek *Leda*. (1980)

NEAR TILBURY LOCK

Above: Northfleet Hope, looking up-river towards Grays. In the centre the *Flinders Bay* - one of the original OCL container ships - lies briefly by the Grain Terminal. On the right the 52,562-ton *Nedlloyd Houtman* waits for the dredger *Arco Tyne* to pass before pulling away from the Container Terminal. (c.1984)

Left: Modern sculpture - looking forward along the shoulder of a *Star* bulk carrier. Such ships, for their cargo handling, rely on travelling gantry-type cranes whose tracks, of necessity parallel, have to extend the whole length of the cargo space. Hence the pronounced overhang seen here. (c.1980)

Right: The Northfleet Container Terminal, with the German *Muscat Bay* (1975/8,475) alongside. Small as container ships go, she carried up to 420 20-ft boxes. Such vessels spend most of their time chartered out to other firms - in this case to OCL - and she was then bearing her fourth name in two years. (1981)

From Tilbury to the Sea

Tilbury Docks, Container Terminal and Landing Stage, Pilot Station, Tug Base, Collier Signal Station, Cliffe, Thames Haven, Coryton, Shivering Sands Fort.

With tugs in attendance OCL's *Flinders Bay* (1969/26,756) makes for Northfleet Container Terminal. (c.1975)

TILBURY DOCKS

The creation of a dock at Tilbury was made necessary by the opening of the Royal Albert Dock in 1880 since that event showed up the shortcomings of the East and West India Docks. Their owners, a rival firm, realised that in order to maintain their position they must build afresh downstream. Construction work at Tilbury began in 1882 and by April 1886 the new dock was ready for business.

Situated about 25 miles below London Bridge and more than halfway to Southend, the dock in its original form, was shaped like the letter E. The long stroke ran nearly east-west and on the north side there were three branches. Altogether 56 acres of water were enclosed, all of it dredged to a depth of 38 ft. Access at a midway point was via a 700 x 80 ft lock at the head of an 18 acre tidal basin. The building of 24 transit sheds, a railway system, two 600 ft-long dry docks and the large Tilbury Hotel raised the cost from an estimated £1.1m to a final £2.8m.

An early lack of customers necessitated lower dock charges and these affected the up-river docks. The financial loss was widespread until an inter-company agreement came into force in 1889. Twenty years later the Port of London Authority was established and this brought unified port control. During the First World War the length of the dock was nearly doubled - to about 1,450 ft - the depth increased and more transit sheds added.

A major event of 1929 was the opening of a new up-river entrance lock. Larger than any ship then afloat, it measured 1,000 x 110 ft. The existing 752 ft-long drydock was retained but the two smaller ones were then filled in. Another contemporary addition was that of a 1,000 ft long riverside cargo jetty. This was followed in 1930 by the opening of the Tilbury Passenger Landing Stage which measures 1,142 x 80 ft.

Developments since the 1960s have been spectacular. The total acreage has been more than doubled by a long dock extension which stretches north-northwest. This caters for containers and ro-ro traffic, the handling of forest products and also general cargo. In the river too - above the entrance lock - there have been two major developments; the creation of the 1,000 ft-long Northfleet Container Terminal and, slightly further up-stream, the Grain Terminal.

In February 1992 Tilbury Docks - now the Port of Tilbury - became privatised after a £32m management-employee buyout.

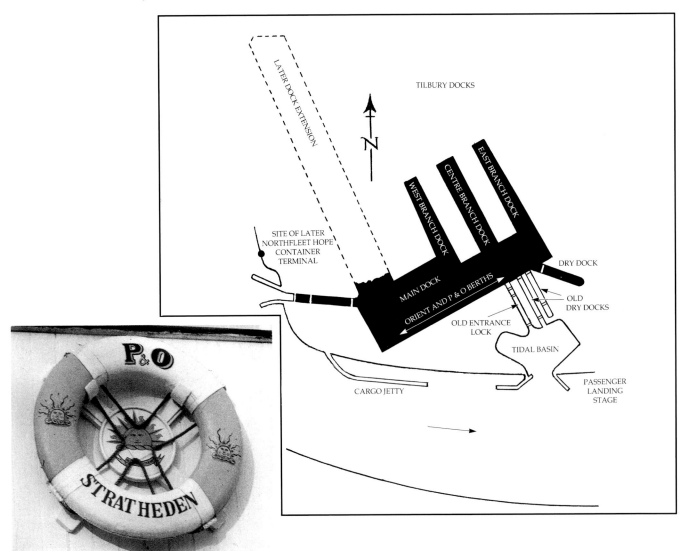

TILBURY DOCKS   *Above:* The Orient liner *Orama* (1924 / 19,840) about to leave Tilbury for Australia. She was then experimentally painted with the corn coloured topsides subsequently adopted for the *Orion* and all new Orient ships. The first of a group of five, she carried first and tourist classes but no third. She was sunk in 1940 by the cruiser *Admiral Hipper* while preparing to evacuate troops from Narvik. (1934)
Below: Tilbury's bascule bridge - now no more - raised to receive the Orient Line's brand new flagship *Orsova* (1954 / 28,790). A 22-knot ship carrying some 680 first- and 810 tourist-class, she was the world's first mastless passenger liner. Transferred to P & O in 1965, she was scrapped nine years later.

TILBURY - THE PRE-WAR ELITE

Left: The Cunard liner *Franconia* (1923/20,340) in white cruising livery. One of a class of five, she lasted until 1956. (1934)

Left: The *Ormonde* (1917/15,047) was the first in the Orient Line fleet to have a cruiser stern and remained their largest until the advent of the *Orama* class of 1924. Her long career ended in 1952. (1934)

Below right: The Red Star flagship *Belgenland* (1917/27,132) - then the largest liner to visit London - in dry dock in Tilbury in 1935. She ended her days as the American *Columbia*.

Below: The P & O Line's *Viceroy of India* (1929/19,628) seen from another liner backing into the lock. The P.L.A. tug is the *Beam*. (1934)

TILBURY AFTER THE WAR

Right: The birth of Tilbury's ro-ro services. The LST *3534* (1945/4,291) just before being renamed *Empire Cedric*. Operated by Frank Bustard & Sons, she ran to and from the Continent carrying equipment for the British Army of the Rhine. (1946)

Centre: The after part of the T2 tanker *Newhall Hills* (1944/10,441) being coaxed into Tilbury lock after her forward portion had been blown off following a collision near the Goodwins. Rebuilt to become the *Afghanistan*, she was sold in 1953 in a fire-damaged state for further trading under the Italian flag. (1947)

Below: The newly renamed *Empire Rest* (1944/1,333) at Tilbury Docks in May 1946. Planned as H.M.S. *Rayleigh Castle*, a 16.5-knot *Castle* class corvette, she was completed instead as a Convoy Rescue Ship.

HOME OF THE PASSENGER SHIPS...

Left: The DFDS passenger ship *Aarhus* (1912/1,843) off the old Tilbury entrance lock in 1946. She and the same company's *Dronning Maud* then sailed regularly to and from the Low Countries.

Above: Two of Tilbury's Australian regulars, the *Oronsay* (1951/27,632) and (right) the P & O *Strathnaver* (1931/22,547), then newly shorn of her two dummy funnels. (1951)

Right: Canadian Pacific's final *Empress*, the *Empress of Canada* (1961/25,780) during her 1972 conversion into the cruise ship *Mardi Gras*.

Left: Although her terraced after decks were a new feature, the layout of the P & O *Iberia* (1954/29,614) differed little from the Orient liners of the mid-twenties.

...AND OF CARGO LINERS

Right: Elder Dempster's *Calabar* (1936/ 8,305) which, over the period 1959-62, sailed regularly between Tilbury and West Africa. Previously the Natal Line's *Umtali*, she carried 100 first class passengers, as did her sister *Winneba* (ex-*Umgeni*).

Centre right: The *City of St Albans* (1943/ 7,264) was one of the twelve Liberty ships bought in 1947 by Ellerman to offset war losses. She served the Company for well over 20 years. (1950)

Below: Half of the *M.I.Okpara*, a 95 ft-long shallow-draught vessel designed for river service in Eastern Nigeria, about to be loaded on the *Kano Palm*. (1976)

Below: The Saudi Arabian *Johara* (1952/7,540) whose name and white, green-topped funnel could not hide her Blue Funnel ancestry. Originally the *Alcinous*, she was one of a series of 21 built between 1947 and 1953. (1976)

VARIETY AT TILBURY

Left: The *Sapele* (1974/9,240) seen preparing for a West African voyage. She was one of a Polish-built series, whose engines-aft layout introduced something new to the Elder Dempster fleet. (1985)

Centre right: The Brazilian *Santo Andre* (1958/3,557) in Tilbury lock as she and her newly offloaded cargo of logs are about to go separate ways. (c.1982)

Below left: The tree which had formed the centrepiece of the *Katsina Palm's* funnel design for 21 years was felled in 1978 when she was sold to become the *New Dragon*. *Bottom*: From hull ribbon to lattice funnel the container ship *Renoir* (1973/13,928) demonstrated the French touch. Others in the Messageries Maritimes series were the *Cezanne, Degas* and *Gauguin*. (1978)

76

THE ADVENT OF RO-RO AND THE BOX SHIP

Right: Ro-ro development: the *Doric Ferry* (1962/2,573) of Bustard's Atlantic Steam Navigation Company which replaced the converted LSTs first used on the Tilbury-Antwerp run. (1962)

Centre left: I'm feeling completely shattered!

Bottom: The *Resolution Bay* (1962/43,995) one of the larger OCL ships loading at 39 Berth. Each such vessel with its size, speed and quick turnaround displaced eight or more conventional cargo liners. (1978)

Centre right: Container ship activity in 1976. From left to right: an OCL *Bay*, the *CP Discoverer*, a Johnson ScanStar ship and the German *Rhein Express*.

MORE BOX SHIPS

Left: Left behind - by some Dockland Cinderella?

Left: Rare sight: while on the East African trade the 18,289-ton *Tarifa* sported both Swedish and Norwegian funnel markings - those of the Transatlantic and Wilhelmsen companies. (1981)

Below: As the Dutch feeder ship *Yolanda* (1978/997) - in from Rotterdam - edges into the lock, a Blue Star container ship manœuvres off the Northfleet Terminal. (c. 1981)

Left and centre: Close-ups of the OCL's first generation container ship *Flinders Bay* (1969/26,756). She and her five sisters boasted a funnel extension quite unique in its shaping. (c. 1975)

Bottom: Extremes of size off Tilbury: the OCL container ship *Resolution Bay* (1977/43,995) being overtaken by the tiny spirit tanker *BP Rapid* (1974/589), (1979)

TRAFFIC OFF NORTHFLEET

Above: Manœuvring off Northfleet: as the deeply laden *La Ensenada* (1974/25,532) leaves and prepares to swing, so the Hong Kong-registered *Star Magnate* (1978/26,925) makes for the vacant berth. (1978)

Below: A small coaster, bound up-river gives scale to the great bulk of the P & O tanker *Ardshiel* (1969/119,678) then making for the Repair Jetty - where she was taken over by new owners. She was 1,063 ft long and had a dead weight tonnage of 214,085 as compared to the 65,000 tons of the *Olympic Challenger* which, in 1960, had been the largest laden tanker to visit the Thames. (1977)

OUTWARD BOUND

Above: Then unique amongst North Atlantic cargo liners in having two funnels, the Cunard Line's *Alsatia* (1948/7,226) and *Andria* ran between London and New York from the early 1950s until their sale to Nationalist China in January 1963. Turbine-driven with a speed of 16-knots, they were first known as the *Silverplane* and *Silverbriar*. (1953)

Below: The British flag *Blenheim* (1970/10,247) of the Fred. Olsen Line - the last passenger firm to regularly use Tilbury Docks - puts on speed as she starts a voyage to the Canaries. A year later - in 1981 - she started a three year period in the Caribbean as the DFDS-owned *Scandinavian Sea*. This ended with a disastrous fire.

'BLUE FLUE' DEVELOPMENT- THREE GENERATIONS

Left: Ancestry unmistakable! The former Glen liner *Flintshire* (1962/11,537) soon after her 1979 sale to become the Chinese *Yang Cheng*. She was one of four (three with *Glen*-names) which were followed by another 21-knot series, the eight-strong *Glenalmond* class.

Centre: The *Patroclus* (1967/12,998) - the former *Glenalmond* - was one of the four which spent their first ten years with the Glen Line before being transferred to Blue Funnel. Outmoded by container ships, they were soon sold. In 1982 the *Patroclus* became the Saudi Arabian *Rajab I* but was scrapped two years later.

Below: One of the next Ocean (Blue Funnel) series, the *Maron* (1980/16,482) in 1982 as the *Studland Bay* while on charter to OCL. Seven of this class were built, four from Japan being followed by three from the Clyde.

OFF GRAVESEND *Above:* With the start of a race imminent, the spritsail barges *Wyvenhoe* (centre) and *Felix* jockey for position in front of the Russian cruise ship *Leonid Brezhnev*. (1986)

Below: Sophistication in banana ships - the handsome and brand-new *Geestbay* (1981/7,730) passes Tilbury Landing Stage bound for the Upper Pool on a publicity visit. Like others in the Geest fleet she has accommodation for 12 first class passengers.

Above: Tide-time contrasts. The inward-bound box ship *ACT I* passes the conventional outward-bound *Glenogle* (right) and her escorting tug *Dhulia*, also the 203-ton Guernsey-owned coaster, *Ord*. (1977)

Centre: With the *Baltika* flying an ensign of Tsarist days and with a contemporary coach nearby, the observer might believe himself in a time-slip. However, it was all for a film on the dancer Pavlova. (1982)

Below: Snap! Exact sisters, the Gearbulk-operated *Alain LD* and, on the right, the *Gerard LD* (both 1974/25,223) pass off the Landing Stage. (1977)

Above: A replica of an early 17th century sailing ship, the *Godspeed*, left London on the 30th April 1985 bound for Jamestown, West Virginia. Her voyage was a re-enactment of that made in 1606-7 which led to the formation of the first successful settlement in America. The vessel, which measured 68 ft. x 14 ft 8 ins started her voyage with a tow from Geenwich to the Isle of Wight.

Below: Christmas Eve overtime at Northfleet as the French bulker *Charles L D* (1979/26,325) loads the last few tons before leaving for Monrovia. (1979)

REMINDERS OF THE OLD

Left: One of the original 'Rabbit Boats', the twin-screw *Saphir* (1897/638) - one of the first merchant ships to have a cruiser stern - at her berth in the Tilbury Tidal Basin. Owned by the Cockerill Line, these ships sailed daily to and from Belgium. (1946)

Centre: The Shell tanker *Darina* (1966/ 39,796) cleaning tanks at the Tilbury Repair Jetty while a local tug joins in the display. (1976)

Below: The newsprint carrier *Phyllis Bowater* (1960/4,040) off the Tidal Basin and old dock entrance. Beyond can be seen the Orient Line's *Orion*. (1976)

ARAB, DUTCH AND GERMAN

Right: Arab armada: the *Ibn Khaldoon* (1976/15,446) was one of 40 similar ships built over a five year period for the United Arab Maritime Company. Of these, half were built on the Clyde, the rest in South Korea. (1978)

Centre: The South Korean-built container ship *Nedlloyd Clarence* (1983/33,405) passing a barge about to be collected by one of the giant Lykes-owned 'Seabee' ships. (1983)

Below: The Belgian-owned, German-chartered *Rhein Express* (1984/32,703) bound for the Northfleet Container Terminal. Now outmoded, streamlining has given way to angularity. (1985)

PRE-WAR CRUISES

Above: The Watkins tugs *Kenia* (left) and *Gondia* handling the German 'Strength Through Joy' cruise ship *Wilhelm Gustloff* (1937/25,484). Torpedoed in the Baltic in 1945 by a Soviet submarine, she sank with the loss of over 6,000 lives. (1938)

Left: After making a round of North Continental ports the Union-Castle Line's *Garth Castle* (1910/7,625) lands her passengers by tender off Gravesend. One of a class of five, she was scrapped in 1939. (1933)

The elegant *Empress of Australia* (1914/21,833) leaving for a cruise in 1933. The former German *Tirpitz*, she earned fame for her rescue achievements during the devastating Yokohama earthquake of 1923.

Above: The 21-knot turbo-electric liner *Strathnaver* (1931/22,270) in her original three-funnelled form. The two dummy ones were removed during her 1948-9 refit. She was the first of the P & O *Strath*-series which were designed for the Australian service and which marked the Company's switch to yellow funnels and white hulls. (1933)
Below: The Zeeland Line's *Koningin Emma* (1939/4,353), alongside the Landing Stage, was then operated to Rotterdam. On the right is the Danish *Friendship* (1934/1,305) - originally H.M.S. *Leith* - then owned by the World Friendship Association. (1948)

FIRST VOYAGE - FINAL VOYAGE

Above: The Orient Line's *Oronsay* (1951/27,632) just before starting on her maiden voyage to Australia. She retained her corn-coloured hull until taken over by P & O in 1962, after which she had all-white topsides. She was finally scrapped in 1975

Right: The Svenska Lloyd *Britannia* (1929/4,216) ready for her final crossing to Gothenburg. Long partnership with her sister *Suecia* was to continue in the Mediterranean, where they operated as the Greek-owned *Cynthia* and *Isthmia*. (1966)

THE GIANT AND THE EVER - POPULAR

Above: For long the largest passenger ship to visit the Thames, the Italia Line's flagship *Michelangelo* (1965/45,911) was designed - like the *Raffaello* - for the Company's Genoa- New York run. Brief use in the cruise trade ended with their sale in 1976 to Iran, where they were used as accommodation ships (1974)

Below: The *Britanis* (1932/18,153), a long-term Chandris favourite, was built as the Matson Line's *Monterey* for the U.S. - Australia trade. Later the *Matsonia* and *Lurline*, she was bought from Matson by Chandris in 1970 and, since 1986, has been cruising in the American market.

OFF ROSHERVILLE   *Above:* Seen a few hours after her ordeal in the Great Hurricane of October 1987, the *Stefan Batory* (1952/15,244) lies alongside Tilbury Landing Stage minus both anchors. Poland's flagship, she was bought in 1969 as the *Maasdam*. Although she later made some cruises, her subsequent standing was summed up by one of her Masters in this fashion: "The last regular passenger liners on the North Atlantic are your great British Queen and a small Polish King". Soon after this final visit to Tilbury she was sold to become an accommodation ship.

Below: A somewhat less popular ship, the Nassau-registered *Astor* (1981/18,834). Built at Hamburg for local owners, she was sold to South Africa in 1983. Shown while bound up-river for Greenwich in 1985, she had then just been bought by East Germany - who changed her name to *Arkona*. A repeat *Astor*, built in 1987, was kept for only a year before becoming the *Fedor Dostoyevskiy*.

Left and below: The *Royal Odyssey* (1964/17,884) of the Royal Cruise Line over the years from 1981 to 1987 made a series of cruises from Tilbury to Baltic ports. Unashamedly one of my two favourite cruise ships, the cluster of lights in her Monte Carlo lounge was typical of her lovely interior.

Below: Typifying the variety and range of sizes handled by River Pilots, the Dutch frigate *Van Speyk* of 2,850 tons displacement appears puny against the bulk of the *Flinders Bay* (1969/26,716) then briefly lying by the Landing Stage. (1982)

FOR LONG THE PILOT'S BASE

Left: The Piermaster of the Royal Terrace Pier, Gravesend, Mr George Oakey, so well known over the years to countless visitors. (1985)

Right: The specially fitted and much-used lookout window with a River Pilot checking the progress of an incoming ship. (c.1978)

Below: The Sea Pilots' old office on the Royal Terrace Pier, an amendment being made to the movements board. (c.1978)

TILBURY - GRAVESEND FERRY

Right: The steam driven *Rose* (1901/259) was the first of a long-lasting Thames-built quartet. The others were named *Catherine, Gertrude* and *Edith.* (1960)

Left: Three on the move in 1962: the vehicular ferry *Mimie* (1924/371) and the 1961-built *Catherine,* also (partly visible) the *Edith.* Beyond is the New Zealand Line's *Remuera.*

Right: The *Catherine* as seen from the *Arkadia* in 1958. Beyond her (on the left) is the vehicular ferry *Tessa* and (right) the *Rose.* In early days the *Catherine* and her sisters would often carry livestock, including flocks of sheep in search of winter grazing.

Left: A crowded Landing Stage with one of the Royal Mail's *Highland* ships about to sail. (c.1950)

Left: The *Tessa* (1924/368) could carry between 20 and 30 cars and 250 passengers. There were sliding doors forward and aft of the superstructure. (1960)

Right: The long-lasting *Edith* (1961/214) nears Gravesend, with her sister *Catherine* in the distance. The Sealink logo was discarded in 1984.

Left: Seen from a different vantage point, the *Rose* (1961/214) passes astern of H.M. Submarine *Finnwhale*, then bound for the West India Docks.

Right: In October 1977 the proposed use of the 35-ton *Humphrey Gilbert* on the Tilbury-Gravesend ferry service proved a pathetic fiasco. A few bumps against the Landing Stage and the base of her life raft collapsed on deck. She was one of a pair built in 1957 for the sheltered crossing between Kingswear and Dartmouth.

GRAVESEND FAMILIARS

Left: The coal hulk *Artemis* which lay off the Promenade from the early 1950s supplied the local tugs - and others - with bunkers. When sold to Medway breakers in 1968 she was the last of her type on the River. Built as the *Borussia* (1912/973) but later named *Timandra*, she was surrendered by the Germans in 1946 and renamed *Empire Confal*. Bought by the G.S.N. a year later, she was used by them as the *Woodwren*. (1967)

Centre: The 55-ton green-hulled *Girl Pat* which, from the late 1940s was used by the P.L.A. as a wreck marking vessel. Years earlier, in 1936, when a new Grimsby trawler, she had been stolen by her skipper who, aided only by a child's atlas, contrived to take her to the West Indies. 52 days out, she was finally arrested at Georgetown, British Guiana. (1947)

Below: The great bulk of the barge-carrying *Doctor Lykes* (1972/21,667) which, with her sisters *Almeria Lykes* and *Tillie Lykes*, used to moor between the two piers. In the winter of 1985-6 all three were sold to the U.S. Military Sea Lift Command. (1975)

TUGS FOR THE BOX SHIP

Right: As an incoming container ship approaches, so the tug *Vanquisher* (1955/294) is the first of three to pull away from the Royal Terrace Pier.

Centre: A line has been passed and the connection made, so one of the three, the *Moorcock* (1959/272), takes up station on the port quarter.

Below: The *ACT 2* and her escorting tugs proceed up-river for the final swinging operation off the Northfleet Container Terminal. (all c.1975)

Left: Upside-down Ns somewhat spoil the overall smartness of the Training Ship *Hanbada* (1975/3,492) of the South Korean Merchant College. (1977)

Above: A more local lapse. (1978)

Below: The French 'box' ship *Kangarou* (1971/26,437) seen from Gravesend Promenade. Her black topsides then looked better than in earlier years when, under Messageries Maritimes ownership, she had her owners' initials (MM) painted along her length - large and bold - and seven times over! Even when photographed she was something of an oddity, her boot-topping being painted blue on the port side and red on the starboard. (1982)

THE PILOT ARRIVES

Below: The steam cutter *Pilot* (1905/39) at work in 1933. The liner has her emergency boat swung out.

Above: The step aboard.

Left: The long climb.

Right: The power assisted hoist.

BELOW GRAVESEND *Above:* The Tilbury collier reporting station preceded the telephone, messengers on horseback being sent from here to London with the latest news of ship arrivals. In the distance is the United States Lines' *American Corsair* (1962/11,105) on her way to the Royal Victoria Dock. (1967)

Below: The British coaster *Con Zelo* (1957/399) on the slip at Denton repair yard, her lines revealing Dutch construction. Owned by Jeppesen Heaton Ltd. she was then unusual in never having been sold or renamed. (1983)

TANKER TRAFFIC

Above: Sun tugs guiding the Onassis tanker *Olympic Challenger* (1960/35,758) to No. 10 Jetty, Thames Haven. A turbine-driven vessel of 65,000 tons dead weight, she was then - in 1960 - the largest tanker to visit the Thames.

Right: The *Methane Princess* (1964/21,876) off Canvey Island. There, up to about 1980, she and a sister discharged about one-tenth of all the gas needed in Britain. This, which came from the Sahara, was loaded at Arzew in Algeria and carried in liquefied form at a temperature of minus 258° F. (1965)

Below: Of all the tanker jetties on the Kentish shore Conoco's at Cliffe is furthest downstream. Alongside is the Liberian *Allison Star* (1960/12,458). Four names earlier she had been built as the *Athelqueen*. (1978)

Above: Then described as one of the world's most costly ships, the brand-new gas tanker *El Paso Paul Kayser* (1975/66,806) shown undergoing tests at Canvey Island. Designed to carry LNG (liquefied nitrogenous gas) she has, in fact, seen very little service.

Left: Far out in the Estuary, some 59 miles below London Bridge and near the limits of its jurisdiction, the Port of London Authority has its Tidal Gauge; this on one of the gaunt looking Shivering Sands Forts of World War 2. Passing by is the coastal tanker *Dublin* (1969/1,077) then owned by Shell-Mex & B P Ltd. (1974)

GO NO FURTHER!

Above: The nearly righted East German *Magdeburg* (1958/6,629) at Broadness in September 1965 with the floating crane *Magnus* alongside. Sunk after a collision with the *Yamashiro Maru* in October 1964, she was subsequently taken to Tilbury and sold. On December 13th she left in tow of the German tug *Albatross*, but sank four days later.

Right: The forlorn bow section of the *Rustringen* (1953/642), a German owner-captained coaster which sank in the lower reaches after a December 1972 collision. The main after section had already been raised and beached.

Below: Competition verboten. The tugs *Daunt Reef* (near) and *Carrig Reef* idle off Higham in 1981 - the sad end to an opposition venture by Reef Tugs which was killed after its first customer was blockaded in Tilbury Docks by seven local tugs. Monopoly and restrictive practices have done nothing to encourage London's trade.

LOCAL EXCITEMENTS

Left: The *Sun Kent* douses a fire on the former Grimsby trawler *Boston Boeing* (1962/707) then being scrapped at Old Sun Wharf. (1980)

Centre: Near dusk at Northfleet Hope in January 1986 the tug *Vanquisher* (1955/294) sinks after being pulled over by the *Jervis Bay's* tow-rope. No lives were lost and the tug later returned to service. Two other major tug occasions involved the *Jervis Bay*. Launched on the Clyde she had to be towed to Germany for completion. Later, as the first of her class to be sold to breakers, she broke from her tug and was wrecked at Bilbao in 1984.

Below: The damaged tanker *Esso Wandsworth* (1943/4,352) at Tilbury in October 1965 with her foremast lying on deck. Bound from Thames Haven for Littlebrook a month earlier, a fog collision forced her to be beached. Refloated, she caught fire and had to be scrapped. One of a U.S. quartet bought in 1956, her sisters were named after *Chelsea, Fulham* and *Lambeth*.

SAILING SHIP CONTRASTS

Right: The handsome barque-rigged training ship *Statsraad Lehmkuhl* (1914/1,701) about to enter the Surrey Commercial Docks. For long owned in Norway, she started her career as the Tecklenborg-built *Grossherzog Friedrich August*. (1969)

Below: The auxiliary schooner *Charlotte Rhodes* of TV fame. Built in 1904 with a length of 115 ft, and fictionally owned by the Onedin Line, she in fact belonged to the Charlotte Rhodes Foundation - until lost by fire in Amsterdam in October 1979. When first seen at Dartmouth in 1972, all her running gear was neatly labelled for the benefit of her actor crew.

FAMOUS EXCURSION AND SAILING SHIPS

Left: Crowds pack the deck of the paddle steamer *Isle of Arran* (1892/513). A veteran of the Clyde (Buchanan) fleet, she was bought by the G.S.N. in 1933 and spent four seasons on the river before being scrapped at Grays. She had a single-cylinder engine and one 'haystack' - type boiler. (1934)

Left: The G.S.N. excursion ship *Royal Sovereign* (1948/1,851) was built by Dennys of Dumbarton and had two Sulzer diesels giving a speed of 19 knots. Long service between Tower Pier and Southend/Ramsgate ended with a season based at Great Yarmouth. Sold in 1967, she then became Townsend's *Autocarrier*. (1956)

Below: Among a summer influx of training ships, the Romanian *Mircea* (1939/1,600 tons displacement) was one of the most handsome. Her length over bowsprit is 267 ft and she carries around 140 midshipmen. Built at Hamburg as the last - and largest - of four, she resembles the *Eagle, Sagres* and *Tovarisch*. (1975)

MORE CONTRASTS IN SAIL

Right: The *Golden Hinde* replica leaving St Katharine's Dock in 1974. She then made a round of British ports before sailing for North America. Built by J Hinks & Son of Appledore, she was launched in April 1973.

Below left: Guests beware, headroom is limited! The same *Golden Hinde* had a waterline length of 75 ft and a breadth of 20 ft. The great amount of tumblehome resulted in an extremely narrow poop.

Below right: A veteran of many ocean voyages, the barque *Lawhill* (1892/2,816) moored off Gravesend in the 1930s. Then owned by Gustaf Erikson, of Mariehamn, she had a registered length of 317 ft. Built by Thompson's of Dundee, she was first owned by the local firm of Charles Barrie.

ALTERNATIVE FATES.

Above: Destined for preservation in the 'States, the barque *Peking* (1911/3,120) passes Gravesend in 1975 after being prepared at Blackwall for her trans-Atlantic tow. Originally a German nitrate carrier, she spent much of her life in the Medway as the training ship *Arethusa*.

Above: Slow disintegration over the years - such was the fate of the ex-Danish auxiliary schooner *Hans Egede* (1922/303) Her trading career over, she was being towed up-river when her seams opened. After hurried beaching she was finally moved to rot at Cliffe. (1980)

Right: Quick destruction for recycling: The bows of the Crawley tank barge *Dutch Courage* being cut up at Old Sun Wharf, Gravesend. Following her purchase from Holland she had been used to carry oil supplies to up-river installations. (1982)

BABEL RULES OK

Some decorative examples of maritime calligraphy including a slight hiccup caused by over-optimism over the space available for one name - and a phonetic *Desert Kink* - er, *King*.

UԵԱԲԼՈ
ԿԼՊԵՂՈՈ1

ХУДОЖНИК ПРОРОКОВ

स्टेट ऑफ मनिपुर
STATE OF MANIPUR
BOMBAY

قطري بن الفجاءة
الــدوحــة

Index to Ship Names